THIS BOO(
PROPERTY OF
KEVIN M. MILLER

Being Real

A Simple Way to Transform Your Life and Ministry!

248.4
Pea
being real

3370
Peart, Brian

Brian L. Peart

PublishAmerica
Baltimore

© 2009 by Brian L. Peart.

All rights reserved. No part of this book may be reproduced, stored in a retrieval system or transmitted in any form or by any means without the prior written permission of the publishers, except by a reviewer who may quote brief passages in a review to be printed in a newspaper, magazine or journal.

First printing

PublishAmerica has allowed this work to remain exactly as the author intended, verbatim, without editorial input.

ISBN: 1-60703-535-9
PUBLISHED BY PUBLISHAMERICA, LLLP
www.publishamerica.com
Baltimore

Printed in the United States of America

Being Real

A Simple Way to Transform Your Life and Ministry!

Being Real!

I had been watching God move in amazing ways in relationships over the last few months and wanted to write about it but I wasn't sure how or what to write about. I couldn't put my finger on the cause of these incredible moments that seemed to be happening more frequently. Moments that were beyond my ability to co-ordinate or foresee. In truth, they were moments where God was moving, it had nothing to do with me. And then, while driving one morning, I heard a terribly sad situation on the Christian radio and all of a sudden, God brought clarity. And the message just came to life. This is a message for Christians in

America. We have a challenge on our hands, but the Lord has given us the victory. I believe that if we, as Christians, embrace the concept in this book, a revival could break out in churches across America. And true healing can begin. I have seen it in my own life, in my own Bible studies and I want you to experience God move in your life, ministry and church as well.

That morning, the DJ on this Christian radio channel, shared that someone had called in the prior day and shared how he had been going to church for 2 years and had no authentic relationships. That even though he was a member of the church, there was no one he could open up to and he still felt alone. What floored the DJ, and the station, and galvanized this message in my heart was the incredible response to that one caller. The DJ said that they had never gotten so many calls and e-mails from people saying they felt EXACTLY the same way. Alone, without true friends. Many said the only true friends they had were the non-Christian friends they knew before getting saved. One guy called in and shared that he was a drug addict and went through recovery and after the recovery has been going to church and 2 years later he still does not have anyone who he can truly open up to. He had more friends, real authentic friends, from the addiction recovery which was 6 months long then he had in 2 years attending a "Community oriented" church. My heart was grieved. Many of those calling in were involved in Baptist churches, or "emerging" churches and even "blowing and going" mega-churches. No church seemed exempt.

Contrast that to Acts 2: "They (the early church) devoted themselves to the apostles teaching and to the fellowship, to the breaking of bread and to prayer... All the believers were together and had everything in common. Selling their possessions and goods they gave to anyone as he had need.

Every day they continued to meet together in the temple courts. They broke bread in their homes and ate together with glad and sincere hearts...." Acts 2: 42-47. Oh yes, and they enjoyed God's favor as the Lord added to their number daily those who were being saved.

Quite a different picture. The early believers were a family-they were tight. They were sincere and real. They experienced everything together- the highs and the lows. What is the disconnect between that time and now? What has gone wrong? And more importantly, how can we fix it?

We Have
Become Islands

I think the answer can be found in those two words-sincere and everything. The believers in the early church spent time together but they shared their joys AND their sorrows-they were sincere. They shared everything-the good and the bad. It is quite different in church today in America. Here is a typical Sunday situation in America (names are fictional and bear no resemblance to actual persons):

John and Sue have 3 kids, they struggle mightily getting them all dressed, teeth brushed and in the car to church. They can't find Junior's shoes and Sue is stressing big time. They get in the car and John has to yell at the kids 3 times on the way to church as little Sally kept pulling Betty's hair and Junior wet his pants. As they pull into the parking lot totally stressed, they see their "good" friends the Johnson's, who are getting out of the car at the same time. They smile, wave, "How are you brother?" says Tom Johnson. "Doing Great" says John. "Us too" says the Johnson's.

John and Sue wonder how come the Johnson's have it all together. They never seem to fight. Of course, what they don't know is that the Johnson's are close to divorce because Tom Johnson loves his career more then his children according to his wife Linda, and Linda just doesn't understand Tom's needs according to Tom. All of them with plastic happy faces, friends in the same small group, totally isolated from each other or any authentic community. We must not just get into relationships and small groups and community and put our best faces on so everyone thinks "better of us". We MUST open up to our fears, our trials and our tribulations-we must be sincere and authentic-if we want to truly start a revival in America.

"No man is an island entire of itself" —John Donne

I think Satan has slowly, over time, gotten Christians to buy into a belief that once they get saved, things will be better. That if they are to be effective they must show how much "better" they are so they can help influence people positively. It is the hidden danger in the prosperity gospel that is so popular today. It continues to put an emphasis on having, doing and being-better, richer, and healthier. So we put on masks, we hide our fears and struggles because we don't want to let people know that we are "failing". The only time they open up is in their quiet time alone with the Lord. The beauty of Jesus is that you can totally open up, totally be real, share your feelings, your struggles, your pain and ask for help. Jesus listens with care and concern. The thing is, God has put the help all around us. But because we are scared to open up, the help never comes-even though it is all around us. And we become an island, more withdrawn in our hidden closets.

Every person in our life God has placed there for a reason but we can not discover that reason unless we open up. Do you see it? We need to take off the mask and get real if we are to experience the fullness of the riches of Christ. The Lord has provided, in the people around us, all we need to live fulfilling and enriched lives. Satan tries to keep us an island unto ourselves, with a phony mask on, because he knows that if we woke up to true authentic relationships, if we banded together in sincere worship like the Acts 2 church, there is nothing he can do to stop the power of Christ. America can be a great bastion of Christianity once again and we can feel and see the power of God everyday—if we will just open up. We must build a bridge between our little islands...there is too much at stake!

It Just Takes One to Start the Bridge!

I am a nationwide trainer and "guru", so to speak, in the mortgage business. During 2007 and 2008, while everyone else in the mortgage business struggled, we exploded. I hold seminars, am asked to speak at conferences, and my company is doing very well. That is now. But from 2002-2004 my business struggled mightily. We were near the brink of bankruptcy and every day I would get on my knees and beg the Lord to help my company. I did everything, worked 12 hour days, sacrificed my relationship with my wife and family. Worse, I hid the struggles from my wife-ashamed and embarrassed that I was not successful. For some reason, men have great trouble taking off the masks yet men MUST lead this charge of authenticity. As long as we stay on our island, revival can't break out, healing can't happen. It was when I came clean and got real that the healing began. In 2005 we turned a profit and then we began to take off in 2006.

About a year ago God taught me something important-I could reach more people and help more people by talking about my near failure then by staying on a pedestal. I do tips every week to over 20,000 mortgage people and I have embraced the fact that the struggle I went through has prepared me to lead others in this trying time in our industry. And this is a GREAT CHRISTIAN TRUTH-the area where you struggle is EXACTLY where your greatest ministry will be. Let me repeat that, your biggest impact, the place where you will help the most people and feel the most fulfilled, is in the area that you struggled or are struggling in the most. But if you never open up to that area-YOU NEVER GET TO REALIZE YOUR FULLEST POTENTIAL. Do you see now why Satan wants you to keep playing a game and wearing a mask? If you open up, God will reach MANY people through you. As I have shared my struggles with the mortgage industry and encouraged them to stick it out, they see that there is a light at the end of the tunnel. I am not some glorified guy that got lucky but a person just like them. Who struggled just like they are now but got out of it. This has led to tremendous ministry opportunities nationwide. OPPORTUNITIES THAT WOULD HAVE NEVER HAPPENED IF I STAYED ON A "GURU" PEDESTAL. It just takes one person to take off the mask and admit the problems for true ministry to break out.

A couple of months ago I was having breakfast with my pastor in GA. We were talking, it was pleasant, and then I shared that it bothered me that my oldest son Zachery likes to be the bad guy in the video games he plays. He chooses to be Darth Vader on Lego Star Wars instead of Luke Skywalker. He is a GREAT kid, don't get me wrong, but I opened up about a fear I had. A simple admission. Immediately my pastor opened up about struggles he is having with his boy who is my son's age and one of my son's best friends. My courage and willingness to open up gave him the freedom to open up. Pastors are put on pedestals and find it very hard to open up. But they are human beings and they struggle-often mightily. Pastor, you NEED to open up to your flock. It just takes one person to open up and true relationships, true healing, true ministry and yes, even revival, can break out. We are fearful that people will think less of us and that it will somehow hinder our ministry but that fear is just that, fear. It is not reality. The truth is, EVERYONE struggles in some area. No one has it all together. We preach that no one is perfect, not even one, yet we are scared to admit that we are not perfect for fear of harming the ministry. Do you see the irony? And worst of all, it limits what God is trying to do in our lives.

I was in Las Vegas doing a conference for mortgage brokers shortly after that meeting with my pastor. I did up fliers and handed them out about a Bible Study I was going to hold in the morning at the restaurant. The first day, 4 people came. The second day, 10. But God was all over that second day, healing and ministry happened and none of the people that went will ever forget it. There in a restaurant in the middle of Vegas, God broke out. It started with a prayer, and then I went through a Bible lesson. There were 2 people that own one of my net branches, 4-6 other people that knew me and looked up to me as a teacher and mentor. And 2 people I did not even know because someone else invited them. After the lesson I opened it up to questions or comments and someone shared something-I don't even remember what it was but the Lord convicted me to admit something openly that I had never really admitted before. Despite the fact that these people looked up to me, that I was the "leader" of that group, and despite my fear, I obeyed the prompting of the Holy Spirit.

I shared with them that in 1999 I accidentally clicked on a link to a porn site and got hooked. I never paid any money, I was WAY too ashamed for that but you can see a lot of stuff for free without spending anything. It was repulsive really. Porn may be socially acceptable now and "no big deal" for some, many episodes of various TV shows even kind of glorify it. But if you are a Christian-you just KNOW in your deepest heart that it is wrong the first time you see it. Of course, the longer you watch it, the less that "guilt" is felt. Kind of like cigarettes, when you first smoke one your body repulses but do it long enough and soon your body craves it. For about 3 weeks I worked late each night-that is what I told my wife. But I was really surfing porn sites. The thing was, I hated it. It repulsed me. I couldn't believe I was doing it, there was incredible guilt. But there was an incredible high that I was getting. I found it hard to stop. But I was terribly convicted and each day I wasted in surfing the web instead of doing what I needed to do, I got more disgusted with myself. By the second week I was praying fervently for God to help me break this thing. By the third week I was done. The conviction was so great I stopped right there, threw the computer away in a sign of cutting the ties to the addiction and never went back again.

What happened next in that Bible Study in Vegas was a Holy Spirit led revival really. The girl across the table from me was losing her husband because he was addicted to porn. I had no idea-but God did. People opened up, they prayed, they cried, they shared. It was real. It was powerful, and none of us will ever forget it. It took just one person, who happened to be the leader, to open up to a transgression and GOD came in. Now follow me, if I had not opened up, everyone would have gone their way, thinking how "nice" the Bible study was but God wanted so much more. He wanted healing, he wanted his power to flow, and all I had to do was open up. I did not have to re-learn anything, everyone can open up, we just need to move through the fear. Minister, small group leader, sold-out believer, CHRISTIAN...listen up. This is CRITICAL STUFF! You MUST be willing to open up to your fears and trials and tribulations if you want to effect real change. If you want to have revival. IT CAN NOT HAPPEN IN PLASTIC, FAKE CHURCHES. God is not there EVEN IF THE NUMBERS ARE GROWING. Many of the people that responded to that DJ at the beginning of this book are people that go to big churches that are "blowing and going". The people are proud of the church, it has an impact in the community. But it is still full of people wearing masks and smiling and waving all nice and pretty-and alone! It is time to GET REAL!

Being Real!

We CAN build a bridge across this gap and the good news is, it could happen quick. A revival can break out, a revolution in ministry in America. It just takes one pastor, one small group leader, one Bible Study teacher to open up and get real. What God does next will ASTOUND you. Your openness will free up others, they will share, people going through the same problems will discover others like themselves all around them. The healing will begin. Soon authentic community will break out. Don't be deceived, most small groups and Bible Studies in America rarely open up in this manner. We are still trying to put on our "show face", afraid that people will look down on us if they knew how much we really struggle.

But it won't be like that. I have been doing this now for a year and the opposite happens. You think people will think less of you but actually they open up and soon they look at you as a leader, a friend, somebody real. Your courage to admit your flaws gives them the freedom to admit theirs and God uses that to bring healing, brokenness, revival, authentic community. It can only happen this way. Remember, your area of greatest struggle is actually where your ministry will have the most impact. If you got thrown in prison for drugs in the past, and you will open up about it, God will allow you to lead many others. I have never been thrown in jail, I am licensed to preach, happily married for 11 years. The guy in the prison won't listen to me-he will say I don't know what it is like. And he is right. But the drug addict who got saved and once was in prison himself can reach that guy. But not if you are afraid to admit your past. I know multiple people who are considering moving far away to "start fresh" because everyone around them, church going people now, won't seem to look past their recent failures. And here brings possibly the most important part of this book...

We Can NOT Cast the First Stone!

In John 8:3-9 we see the story of a prostitute about to be stoned for her sins by the Scribes and Pharisees and brought to Jesus. Jesus bends down, begins writing, and challenges the person who is without sin to throw the first stone. Maybe he was writing the various sins in the sand that the many people were guilty of, who knows. But what we do know is that one by one the people dropped their stones and left. Until there was none left but Jesus. Listen, we are ALL guilty of sin. We all fall short. If someone is broken or brave enough to admit their struggles or fears there is only one response that the Christian should have-compassion and love. God is already dealing with them, for you or I to then condemn them when they are reaching out is a grievous mistake. Woe to that person on judgment day who casts that first stone to the broken person.

I am not talking about pointing out a sin-that is not judgment. If a brother confides in me and says he is thinking of cheating on his wife and I tell him that is adultery and it is wrong and he should not do it-that is not judging, that is speaking truth. That is totally different then a brother coming to me, opening up that he has cheated in the past, feels horrible and doesn't know what to do. That is a brother reaching out. Jesus treated all such people with love-it was the hypocrites he blasted. The ones who hide behind their masks and cast stones at the "sinners", when they themselves are racked in sin. In this short book I have admitted something that I am very embarrassed about.

People that look up to me will read this. My mother will read this, my family, my wife's family. What they do with that information I can not control. But I have seen enough of this to know that God will work through it. They won't condemn, God will use it to transform.

We hesitate to admit such things because we fear what people will say but the truth is-you are only responsible for the effort-GOD is responsible for the results. God will work in it. Good will come from it, ministry will happen, revival will break out-lives will be changed. Only in our openness and brokenness can God truly work. So husband, open up to your wife on what you are struggling with. Wife, tell your husband your fears.

Their initial reaction may not be what you hoped, remember, they are human and our knee jerk reaction is often the wrong one. But they will quickly adjust. Once my wife really found out that our business was in the toilet, once I truly got real, she was initially mad. But she was more upset that I waited so long to open up. And a couple of hours later, she adjusted to the reality and became supportive. And our relationship is stronger today than it ever has been.

Father, don't be afraid to let your kids know you are human and you make mistakes. I spoke with one dad who was still trying to be the "perfect" dad to his little boy. When they are young, those kids think you hung the moon. And we like that adulation. But unless you are real, you are setting up all sorts of problems for that child. How else will they learn that failure is OK and a necessary prerequisite to success if you hide all your failures? If you never admit you are wrong, how are they to learn how to be in real relationships. I remember the day my parents got divorced-I was 12. It hit me like a ton of bricks because we had no idea there was anything wrong. They hid everything. Now they were trying to protect us, and did what they thought was right. And my mom did a great job as a single mom with three kids after that and we all turned out OK. But to this day I am still learning how to effectively communicate with my wife when we disagree because I never saw my parents disagree. Kids learn from watching so if you hide it, they don't learn. If give and take does not exist for parent and child, how will that child learn give and take in the important relationships down the road like marriage? There is no real downside to opening up, only healing and the potential for true authentic relationships. Pastor, open up to your congregation, they need to know you are real. Small group leader, open up to that group and watch as others do the same. All we need is all around us if we just open up.

CHRISTIAN, wherever you are, whatever group you are in, stand up and be the leader. Be the person God called you to be. Be bold and unafraid to open up. The Bible says the "Fear of man is a snare" (Proverbs 29:25). So step out, be bold and move without fear. And then watch as one person after another opens up. Watch as God moves and people all around you that are struggling with the same thing come forth. Soon the healing will begin, the revival will start. God will move and move powerfully IN YOUR LIFE AND OTHERS. You will quickly find healing all around you. You will see His powerful hand working all around you and feel a peace, an awe, and a completeness as you finally step square into the center of God's will for your life. And you will begin to realize the full ministry God is calling you too. You will finally find God's will for your life.

If every small group, every Bible study just had one person stand up and open up, there would be an explosion of authentic love. The body of Christ would be revived. Churches would transform and a revival unlike any other would break out and tens of thousands will be saved. Lives will be transformed. And it all starts with one. AND THAT IS THE BEST PART. This is not some "kit" or method we need to learn and teach. This is not a program. It is easy to do. If done together, if each small group would have just one person stand up and open up, the entire church body would transform in days-not weeks. It is stunning what God can do in the heart of a true believer who opens up, gets real, and allows others in. Will you stand up, Christian? Pastor? Small group leader? Husband? Father? Wife? If you will open up, if you will be bold, if you will step out without fear and share your struggles, your pain, your fears then God will honor it and America-and the world-will never be the same. My challenge to you is to be that one! Will you rise to the challenge?

It just takes one.

Printed in the United States
134810LV00001B/186/P